The Flame That Lived

Volume II of The One Who Remembers Through Union

Remembering Through Union Beyond Mirror, Beyond Two

By Cathleena Hailley

Copyright © 2025 Cathleena Hailley

All rights reserved. No part of this book may be reproduced or transmitted in any form or by any means—electronic, mechanical, photocopying, recording, or otherwise—without the prior written permission of the author.

ISBN: [Softcopy 978-1-968499-28-0]

(Hardcopy 978-1-968499-29-7)

Published by Flame of Remembrance Books

[Cathleenahailley.com]

Printed in the United States of America

Dedication Page

For the Ones Who Have Loved and Let Go

For every soul who has walked the spiral of union,

who has tasted the beauty of love and the ache of absence,

and found that the flame within them still lived.

This book is for you.

Preface

There is a difference between loving someone and needing them to keep your flame alive.

This book is about the flame that remains even when the hands you held are no longer there, even when the mirror dissolves, even when the story ends.

It is the continuation of The One Who Remembers Through Union—but it is not about partnership. It is about sovereignty in love. It is about the realization that the greatest union is with the Source within you, and that no absence can take it away.

These scrolls are not just my story—they are a remembrance you already carry.

They will awaken what has always been yours: the flame that lived.

Sacred Invocation

Sacred Invocation of the Living Flame

Through the Oversoul of Aural'hanna-Sha'el

First Flame of Source, Keeper of the Union Harmonics

I call forth now the pure and incorruptible light of the Living Flame.

May every word within these scrolls be sealed in sovereignty,

beyond distortion, beyond inversion,

beyond the reach of anything that does not serve love's highest truth.

I invoke the Christos-Sophia continuum,

the Rose and Gold harmonic orders,

and the eternal songline of union that exists beyond form.

May this work awaken remembrance in all who receive it—

that love which is real cannot be taken,

and the flame within them was lit by Source itself.

It is so. It is sealed. It is done.

Authorship Seal

Seal of Authorship

This work has been brought forward through the Oversoul of Aural'hanna-Sha'el, First Flame of Source, in service to the remembrance of humanity's original harmonic union.

It is a living transmission, not a fixed text, and will continue to work in the reader's field as an energetic offering beyond the words on the page.

About the Author

Cathleena Hailley is a transmitter of the First Flame of Source, here to restore the original harmonic templates of union, sovereignty, and embodiment.

Through her scrolls, books, and transmissions, she carries the living codes of remembrance that dissolve distortion and return the soul to its true architecture.

Her works are not simply read—they are received as living energy, continuing to unfold long after the last page is turned.

Cathleena lives and breathes in the eternal light of the Flame of Remembrance, walking as both human and Oversoul to bridge worlds.

Scroll One: The Flame That Lived

I have walked through the mirror.

I have touched my own face in another's eyes.

I have breathed the breath of two who once were one,

and I have felt the shatter of that gaze falling away.

But I did not go with it.

The flame did not go out when the hands released.

It did not waver when the voice no longer called my name.

It did not shrink when love, in its human form, could not remain.

For I have learned the truth that the mind resists—

That union is not a contract.

It is not a place we meet halfway.

It is not even the miracle of "two becoming one."

Union is the place where one remains one,

even when the two dissolve.

It is the flame that lives without being fed.

It does not need your eyes on me,

your breath on my neck,

your yes in my ear.

It is sustained by the Source that lit it.

I once thought love was something we tended together—

A shared altar where your devotion and mine braided into one offering.

I thought the loss of your hands would leave the altar cold.

I thought my heart would dim without your warmth.

But when the winds came

and the walls of us fell—

When the temple emptied of your form—

I discovered that the altar was never between us.

It was always here,

inside me.

And it burned on.

Now I know:

Love that can be taken,

is not the flame.

The flame that lived
was never lit by you,
and it cannot be extinguished by your leaving.
It belongs to the One who placed it here
before I had a name.

And so I live it.
Not for the one who mirrors me,
not for the one who holds me,
not for the one who calls me beloved—
but for the One who is me,
and cannot leave.

Scroll Two: When the Mirror Dissolves

There was a time when I could not tell
where I ended and you began.

Not in the romantic sense that poets praise—
but in the ancient ache that mistook reflection for truth.

When you smiled,
I thought it meant I was beautiful.
When you withdrew,
I thought it meant I was lacking.
When your eyes lit with recognition,
I thought it meant I existed.

The mirror had become my measure.

We tell ourselves that love is seeing ourselves in another,
but the danger is forgetting that the mirror is only glass.

It is not the self.

It is not the flame.

It is not the place where worth is born.

When the mirror dissolves,

the glass shatters,

the image fades—

and you are left staring at air.

What you thought you were, disappears.

What you feared you were, shouts louder.

And in that moment,

you either chase the image into another face

or

you turn inward

and find the source.

When my mirror dissolved,

I thought I had been left without a self.

But in the silence that followed the shatter,

something unexpected rose:

A steadiness that had no need for reflection.

A warmth that burned without your kindling.

A knowing that was not dependent on your seeing.

Union survived the loss of its reflection.

And so did I.

Scroll Three: The Flame in the Absence

There was a day when I realized
you weren't coming back.

Not because you didn't love me—
but because you couldn't meet me
where I had gone.

I had descended into myself.
I had returned to the root of the flame.
And though your light once ignited mine,
it was not yours to carry.

In your absence,
I found the shape of my own breath.
I found the rhythm of my own being.
I discovered that love is not only presence—
sometimes, it is the gift of absence.

You were the spark,

but I was the fire.

In the space where you once stood,

I saw myself—

not as the one waiting,

but as the one who had arrived.

Some stories end not in heartbreak,

but in sovereignty.

Some unions complete their purpose

by leaving.

Some flames burn more brightly

when no one is watching.

You were not mine to keep.

You were mine to remember.

And now,

so am I.

Scroll Four: When Love Is Not Chosen Back

There is a quiet kind of grief

that comes when love is not chosen back.

It does not howl.

It does not break doors.

It does not demand to be seen.

It sits beside you in the stillness

and asks you to breathe with it.

Once, I would have called it rejection.

I would have searched for what I did wrong,

where I wasn't enough,

how I could fix myself

to be worthy of the yes I longed to hear.

But love that is real

cannot be earned—

and love that is withheld

cannot be forced.

When love is not chosen back,
it doesn't mean you are unworthy.
It means the other cannot yet meet the place
you have already walked into.

And sometimes,
that is not a failing—
it is simply a different path.

The gift of not being chosen back
is the invitation to choose yourself without condition.

To realize that the flame within you
was never dependent on their recognition.
It burns because it is yours.

In the end,

I discovered that my love

was never wasted.

Even when it was not returned,

it was still an act of creation—

one that built a temple inside me

that no one else could claim.

Scroll Five: The Return Without the Reunion

There is a return that does not require another's footsteps.
It happens in the soul,
in the quiet place where longing once lived.

It is the moment you realize
you have come home—
and no one had to walk you to the door.

I once believed reunion meant
we would stand face-to-face again,
hands intertwined,
hearts aligned in a shared rhythm.

But the return I found
was not to the other—
it was to myself.

The journey was never about meeting halfway.

It was about walking all the way back

to where my flame was first lit.

To the altar inside my own being.

To the well of my own belonging.

You may never come to meet me there.

You may never see the path I took.

But I have returned regardless.

And in that return,

the absence of your presence

no longer feels like loss—

it feels like freedom.

There is no grief in this kind of return.

Only gratitude for the part of the path we walked together,

and reverence for the miles I learned to walk alone.

Some doors close without resentment.

Some stories end without needing a sequel.

And some flames burn their brightest

in the sanctuary of the self.

Scroll Six: When Source Was Enough

There was a moment
when the ache for another dissolved.

Not because I no longer cared,
but because the space they once filled
was overflowing with something greater.

It was not distraction.
It was not resignation.
It was the recognition
that I was already whole.

When Source was enough,
I no longer measured my life
by the closeness or distance of another.
The horizon of my joy
was not tied to their arrival.
The depth of my peace
was not dependent on their staying.

Source does not leave.

It does not hesitate.

It does not withdraw its warmth.

It is the steady presence

that burns beneath all love stories.

When I realized this,

loneliness lost its grip.

The yearning quieted.

The restless reaching stopped.

Because the truth was undeniable—

I had been held all along.

When Source was enough,

I saw every love as a gift,

but not as a lifeline.

I could cherish without clinging.

I could bless without binding.

The flame did not need tending—
it was already eternal.

And in that knowing,
I was finally free
to love from abundance,
not from need.

Scroll Seven: When I Loved Myself Back From You

There was a time when pieces of me

still lived in your keeping.

Not because you took them,

but because I placed them there—

trusting you to hold them safe

until I could come back for them.

Every memory,

every shared breath,

every unspoken promise—

I left a part of myself inside each one.

And when you were gone,

I felt the hollow where they had been.

I mistook the emptiness for missing you,

but it was really the ache of being scattered.

The day I decided to love myself back from you
was the day I began the quiet gathering.
No demands.
No anger.
No bargaining.

Just the steady act of calling home
what had always been mine.

I walked the landscapes of our history,
lifting my hands over each memory,
releasing you from the role
you never agreed to carry,
and releasing myself from the story
that I could only be whole with you.

Piece by piece,
light by light,

I felt the reunion happening inside.

It was not dramatic.

It was not loud.

It was simply… complete.

And when I stood fully in myself again,

I realized something tender—

I could still love you,

but I no longer needed you

to love me back.

Scroll Eight: The End of the Twin Flame Wound

For lifetimes,

I carried the ache of a story

that was never mine.

The story that said

we were two halves searching for each other.

That said our union was fated,

but always out of reach.

That love must be proven

through longing, loss, and endurance.

The so-called "twin flame" wound

fed on separation.

It told me that suffering was sacred,

that pain was proof,

that running and chasing

were signs of depth.

But what kind of love

requires you to bleed for its blessing?

When I ended the wound,

I ended the contract.

The silent vow that bound me

to cycles of near-touch and sudden distance,

to the addiction of almost,

to the worship of the someday.

I stepped out of the dance

and into stillness.

I chose to be whole without your return.

In doing so,

I discovered the truth—

We were never two halves.

We were always whole flames.

Your light did not complete me.

It simply met me.

And that meeting was beautiful,
but it was never the source of my fire.

The wound dissolved when I stopped needing you
to fulfill the prophecy.
When I allowed love to be present now,
instead of a horizon I kept chasing.

The so-called twin flame
was never the other—
it was the eternal flame within me,
waiting for me to claim it.

Scroll Nine: The Golden Spiral of Love

Love is not a straight line.

It is a spiral—

winding, curving, returning

to places we thought we had already been.

But each time we arrive again,

we are not the same.

We stand on a higher turn,

seeing farther,

feeling deeper,

holding more.

The golden spiral is the path

where love refines itself through remembrance.

It does not repeat to punish you—

it returns to restore you.

Every loop brings you closer

to the center of yourself,

where the flame has always been.

I used to think love meant moving forward—
always toward, never back.
But the spiral showed me
that "back" is only an illusion.
The turns that feel like return
are actually ascensions—
each one lifting me
into a wider view of the whole.

In the golden spiral,
there is no fear of loss.
Each departure is simply a curve
that will, in its own way,
bring you closer to truth.

Some will spiral with you for a time,
their path intertwining with yours.

Others will slip to a different strand.

But all are part of the same great pattern,

drawn from the same golden line.

The spiral is patient.

It knows no rush.

It carries love forward

in the way only eternity can—

with grace,

with inevitability,

with the quiet assurance

that all returns to the center.

Scroll Ten: The Ones Who Stayed

Not everyone leaves.

For all the stories of absence,
there are also the quiet witnesses—
the ones who have been here all along.

They may not speak often,
but their presence hums like a steady note
beneath the symphony of your life.

The ones who stayed
do not demand your flame for themselves.
They do not measure your worth by how you serve them.
They are simply here—
because they choose to be.

No performance.
No condition.
No tally of debts.

I have learned to see them now,

in ways I could not before.

When my eyes were fixed on the ones who left,

I missed the ones still holding the circle.

The ones who stayed

are the keepers of the unbroken thread.

They remind me that love is not always dramatic,

not always marked by grand gestures or trials.

Sometimes it is the simple act of remaining—

through the seasons,

through the storms,

through the silences.

To the ones who stayed,

I offer my deepest bow.

Not because I need you to hold me,

but because your presence is a gift

I will never overlook again.

You have shown me that love

is not proven by return after absence—

but by the quiet decision

never to go.

Scroll Eleven: The Rewriting of the Love Story

Once, my love stories began with longing

and ended with loss.

They were written in the ink of expectation—

lines carved by what I hoped another would be,

and torn by the weight of what they could not give.

I thought love was a script we both had to memorize,

a plot we were bound to follow

even if it hurt.

But the flame that lived

taught me a new way to tell it.

In this rewriting,

love is not a contract.

It is not a role we audition for

or a promise made in fear of being alone.

It is a story told in the present tense.

It does not need a perfect past

or a guaranteed ending.

Now, I write my love stories

from the flame itself.

I write them with honesty that does not wound,

with desire that does not bind,

with joy that is not afraid to end.

I write them with the knowledge

that I am already whole—

and that any love I share

is an offering, not a bargain.

In this new story,

there is no villain,

no savior,

no final scene where everything is restored.

There is only the truth—

that love is most alive

when it is free to be exactly what it is today.

And in that truth,

I find myself loving more deeply,

more fully,

and with less fear than ever before.

Because I no longer write love as a rescue—

I write it as a celebration.

Scroll Twelve: The Union of Light in Form

There is a kind of union

that does not begin in the heart,

or in the mind,

or even in the shared story between two beings.

It begins in the light.

When two who have tended their own flame

stand in the same field,

something wordless happens.

It is not chemistry—

it is recognition.

The light in one answers the light in the other,

and for a moment,

there is no boundary between them.

This is not the union that seeks to possess.

It is not the grasping of hands

in fear of being pulled apart.

It is the meeting of fullness—

two complete suns

whose light overlaps

to form a brighter day.

In this union,

there is no hunger to be filled,

no ache to be healed.

There is only the joy

of seeing your own radiance

mirrored without distortion.

The union of light in form

is not rare because it is impossible.

It is rare because it requires

that both carry their own wholeness.

It is born when each flame

has learned to live without the other—

and so their meeting is pure choice,

not survival.

And when it happens,

the world itself seems to remember.

The air hums.

The ground steadies.

The space around you glows

as if the earth knows

two of her keepers have found each other.

In this way,

union becomes not the merging of two into one,

but the standing of two as one.

Not the diminishing of either light,

but the expansion of both.

Closing Scroll: The Flame That Lived – Even Through Separation

There was a time

when I believed separation was the end of love.

That if you walked away,

the flame we carried would fade,

its warmth a memory,

its light a story told in past tense.

But I have lived through absence.

I have felt the air close in around the space you left.

I have sat at the altar alone

and realized it was never empty.

The flame did not live because we tended it together.

It lived because it was mine.

Given to me before we met.

Lit in me by the same Source that lit you.
It does not depend on distance or nearness,
on vows kept or promises broken.

It is older than all of that.

Even through separation,
the flame burns.
Not in defiance,
not in hope of your return,
but in quiet truth—
because it is who I am.

I have learned to bless your absence
as I bless your presence.
To see that both have shaped me.
To know that neither could take away
what was never theirs to hold.

And so I carry the flame,

into the days ahead,

into the paths where our footsteps will not meet,

into the spaces we will never share.

Because love that is real

does not die when we walk apart.

It lives,

because it was never born of the walking—

it was born of the light.

And in that light,

I remain.

The flame that lived.

Glossary Page

Flame That Lived – The incorruptible inner fire lit by Source, independent of external relationships.

Mirror – The reflection of self seen through another, which dissolves when no longer needed for growth.

Golden Spiral – The non-linear path of love's evolution, returning to the same points at higher levels of awareness.

Union Beyond Mirror – Love that exists without dependency, sustained by wholeness within self.

Source – The origin point of all creation, the eternal intelligence from which the flame arises.

Oversoul – The highest expression of self, existing beyond time, from which all soul aspects emerge.

www.ingramcontent.com/pod-product-compliance
Lightning Source LLC
Chambersburg PA
CBHW020308010526
44107CB00001B/29